WE ARE WANDERERS

WE ARE
WANDERERS

HANNAH ELIZABETH KING

"Inner Child" first appeared in Floralkin.com

Cover art: © 2023 by Sara Weintraub
Editor: Chelsey Clammer
First paperback edition: Smartpress.com

ISBN:979-8-218-25103-1

To my soul,
and to all the poet hearts who
see worlds within worlds.

TABLE OF CONTENTS

"Keep walking, though there's no place to get to.
Don't try to see through the distances.
That's not for human beings. Move within,
but don't move the way fear makes you move.

Walk to the well.
Turn as the earth and the moon turn,
circling what they love.
Whatever circles comes from the center."

Rumi

INTRODUCTION

This book of poetry is a chronological testament to life's wanderings. It is an unearthing and restoration, holding my life to the light in acknowledgement and honor. Where the earth is turned and cleared, I replant seeds of native species and pollinator gardens; where the ground lays fallow, I witness what blooms through the seasons, the wild things.

Ten years ago, I stood in an airport terminal waiting for my flight to take me to the South Pacific when I knew I would write a book. The title came to mind in a flash, and I thought, *this is what it is going to be.* I wrote much during my time living abroad. It was a season of expansive beauty, soul searching, deep questioning, religious upheaval, and grief. From that point forward, I kept living the adventure, the heartbreak, and I kept writing poems.

This is the journey, the story of my inner world woven with the outer. A decade of exploring all that I carried with me—the emotions, questions, reflections—as I walked from girlhood into becoming a woman, the evolution of daughter to mother.

The child is always with us. My core memories as a young girl, at seven, eight years old, sitting alone in a meadow beside the oak with pen and paper, noticing the sky and the sounds, climbing the pine tree–at the time, I didn't logically understand the importance of this but I knew it was where I wanted to be. I see now, that was a picture of my soul's essence; I was living my truth. Here I am, thirty-six years old, rediscovering what I knew then.

Looking back, I can see how circles weave and the web of connections form through the years. I didn't imagine that the future book I saw in my mind's eye would be poetry; I assumed I would write a novel or memoir. Last year, through a season of health issues that had me sprawled out on the ground every morning, I would lay under the plum tree in my back field, desperate for rest and reprieve from fatigue, and I experienced something profound. I didn't want to leave the sun's warmth, the wind's breath, the earth's solid body under my spine. I welcomed the company of ants and spiders who dared to walk my skin. I was content, at ease, wanting for nothing but the present moment I was in. Here, doing absolutely nothing in the arms of the natural world, I reconnected with my soul, the unconditional love and presence I had long ago disregarded and forgotten. This relationship began to grow within me, and words began to pour like a spring of water, poetry filled me and overflowed onto pages. I couldn't stop writing, cadenced lines became my spark and flame of life-force; it was the only energy that felt renewable in my weak body. This is when the book manifested into tangible form. I had a decade's worth of writings that I began to compile into a cohesive chronological collection, starting with my earliest work, finishing with the most recent poems I was writing everyday as I navigated the healing process. The final poem in this book was written on my birthday of this year, a sacred monument signifying the closure of a ten-year chapter. As you read these pages, you are following a journey through many landscapes. My hope is you can feel the process—the rolling hills, the valley, the mountain climb, the summit and down again. The collection is in nature's order, the unfolding path of my life as it was written.

For me, there is no separation between healing and poetry. Forced to be still, unable to be actively doing, learning to be present in my physical pain also brought me into presence with my emotional pain, and I found that the body, soul, and spirit each speak a language. I began listening and transcribing. Presence also lends itself to seeing beauty and accessing and receiving love in all forms. Wonder grows, miracles are witnessed, the mysteries of life begin to whisper and sing when there is a willing surrender to uncertainty.

The discovery is our nature. I would say it parallels, but it is so much more than that—all of nature outside of us saturates and contains it. The land, the waters, the universe, this journey is a wandering within all space, an exploration of the expanse without any certainty of where it will lead or what we will find, but what can happen here is relationship—with the wild places, the true nature, both in and around us.

Everything alive expresses itself, and the manifestation of being alive can be seen in cyclical growth and death. The best poetry holds what is buried and brings it to the light, revealing through signs and symbols, words and rhythm what has been internalizing out of sight. It sings the underworld, the inner layers—so do plants and animals, soil and water. Do you feel distinctly removed and separate from the earth? You are not. We are the seed. The seed is us.

We are living poetry.

Through the valley
I roam, a wanderer—
treading between
lavender hues clothed
on mountain ranges,
pink skies blushing
with the sun in its rising.
I hear the voice of one
who calls in whispers,
in stillness,
you are my child,
follow me.

We Are Wanderers

My Dear,

Let us gather all
our precious stones
and take count,
holding light when it greets us,
as it spills onto our faces,
into our eyes,
through our chests.

When we bathe in tender looks
and upward parting lips,
when words crown our heads
in golden adoration—
let us not forget

how costly this worship,
our love.

Precious Stones

Fingers were petals,
palms, leaves,
your arms grew branches
around me.
Blades of grass
we withered,
burnt, blew away,
back to seed, back to dust.

We Are Flowers

Hands in fists,
lips pressed tight
the same way
I was born.
Flushed red
and burning,
choking breaths
becoming gurgling
cries longing for
something more
to feed the hunger,
to feel the warmth
of drowning
in my mother's love.

Drowning In My Mother's Love

The house on the hill
was not our promise.
We made binds
to unearthly dwellings,
beyond breath, beyond flesh
we inhabit one another.
Look at me,
make your entrance
through these eyes
and find your covering
within these hands.
Hold me.
My home will always
be our love.

What We Build

Creature of fear
with trembling hands
and pacing arrhythmic heart.
Eyes unlit, shadow in forms,
bent and kneeling,
praying in the dark.

Creature of Fear

There is a fire in this house;
a raging, fuming beast
swallowing you
and her
from the inside
in the wake of our young eyes.
Never mind the tears,
we burn with our mouths shut tight.

House Fire

You weigh heavy on me,
stone and mortar
laid tirelessly on my chest.
With every brick
and what you have built
slowly, over time,
covering the tender places,
I will bear it.

You Weigh Heavy On Me

On a Monday
before spring,
we dug a hole
deep beneath the oaks,
where we buried
the horse in the ground.

It was cold.
Our boots damp
in soil and stone,
we shivered and cried,
counting the graves
of ones we wanted to love
but lost to the passing of time.

Burial

My fierce creature—
I pet you,
coddle you,
pretend you are tame
all day long calling you names,
my delightful, my loveable...
while you sink your teeth
into my hand,
drawing blood,
remaining the beast
you are and do I
put you down?

My Fierce Creature

As fire she came
in amber leaves,
turning trees to gold.
The red earth moaned,
burning for it's rooted,
silt and clay,
keeper of heat,
of blood and bone
and rivers.
As wind she came
through breathing,
bringing flame
and spreading
blue light, glowing hot
through layers of wood,
flushed skin and vein,
turning hearts to gold.

Alchemy

My mother is a palace of secrets,
walls erected in another time,
marble and stone.
Spiral staircases inside
leading to corridors
of rooms shut tight,
doors locked by brass keys.
I wonder if it began in the womb,
her mother building dreams
in her mind, sketches on paper—
the grand architecture of a daughter.
Her father nodding in agreement,
overseeing designs and revision,
finalizing decisions.
I imagine they started this—
but who came and went,
layering materials in mortar,
carving the finishing details,
raising pillars, furnishing rooms
and filling closets like storehouses?
What life was lived within these walls?
She closed the doors
and locked them,
I do not pretend
to know her.

My Mother Is A Palace of Secrets

You are a beckoning sea,
a body deep and hidden
in itself, calling—
I hear you.
In this summoning,
I am bound to the longing
for your presence.

Commanding attention,
I am feeble, insubstantial
under such authority,
influenced and drifting
toward your voice,
I am a wanderer.
You will find me;
you find me every time.

If I followed the call,
if I was there,
I would be at your feet,
you would meet me,
a steady rise and fall
and reaching—
then retreating.
Stepping forward
you would fold me
slowly into layers,
and *carry me away.*

Mystery lies within you,
I cannot search it out.
Expanse stretching,
touching the horizon,

a brooding sky above,
you are dark and light,
engulfing and reflecting.

In awe of your power,
powerless in your grasp,
who am I to be so close,
who am I to be so near you?
You stand constant,
though you move
and change from
tempest to calm,
you return and bring me
to your side.
How do you know me
the way you do?

Our strength is
nothing to compare.
I am delicate,
you are raging,
bellowing as you cast your
waves up, tossed and beating.
You disperse and I am left
breathless in your watch.
Weakened and needing,
my eyes will not let you go,
You contain all of me.

We both hold secrets
buried deep,
unsettled by the unseen,
it is here

that I can touch you,
know a little of you.
Connected in
the uncertainty,
a natural force of passion
and beauty, endlessly
bordered by land and sky.

Standing at the shoreline,
before the tide,
I throw myself into you
because you can hold me.
My whole being pours
out, all its fear and questioning,
all my yearning—
you wash me away
in a moment.
The taste of salt
on my tongue,
a rush of sweet air,
striking cold across
my face, water and wind,
an intrusion, and I am
at your mercy.

Beckoning

My body is in your hands,
held tightly as you pour me lightly
out of containment.
Cracked skin spills what is within
with the turn of your arm,
the touch of your palm
and slowly,
I become an emptied vessel.

Empty Vessel

I saw your face in a vision;
a moment impermanent
permanently remembered,
in it, joy weaved with sorrow
overwhelming, bringing
me to weep.
What you were,
were not lines drawn
rendering our likeness
or features specific,
unmistakable,
you were a brief flood of love,
uncontainable.
A waterway of life into
what already exists,
my breath swept
and my beating heart quickened
in rapids of confidence carrying
questions in the flow—
this is who you will be,
if I let you.
Present here now,
we could be together.
What we know will transform
familiar into unrecognizable
and uncertain.
You will carve a path through stone
and shape time to create
a landscape entirely different,
if I let it.
I hold to the promises of you,
the way you met me
in a passing glance

at my mind's eye,
and I hold on to
the love that believes
and hopes and love
that covers all,
even my fear,
the doubts and desires
that tense my palms
into fists closed,
unwilling to let go.
I allow my hands
the openness to hold you,
my heart,
the freedom
to love more than myself.

April 28, 2013

If my womb was the moon,
it would be full tonight.
In the darkest blue a light rises
over mountains and rests on me.
I am the chosen one
to bear the weight of a life of wholeness,
to dream the dreams of fathers and mothers.
In hours of shadows and sleep
I keep visions of magic
and dancing in the white of midnight.
I cry for this phase—
for patterns of earth and sun unknown to me.
Hidden secrets orbit,
illuminating amidst dark and space.

My Womb Is the Moon

What does it mean
when two wake
from sleep
with a word
and a feeling,
a presence
of spirit
and an image
of your face?
We hold hands
on the first morning snow
and utter it aloud,
Legacy, I say.
Yes! Legacy, he replies.
Walking through white,
breathing what night
brought to us
and our hearts beat
to what's right.
Here we are,
listen—silence.
The sound of stillness speaks
without words
and sometimes
in lyrics.
What does it mean?

First Snow In February, I Dreamed of You

We wear our love
like an old blanket—
comfortable for sleep,
but it doesn't keep
the heat.

Worn

It burned a hole
through me,
the spark we made,
a one-sided flame.

Fire Starter

My lips move your name
around without a sound.
There is silence in each letter
flowing from my tongue
and what I cannot say aloud
still cries out.

Secrets

Tracing lines around
last night's dreaming—
fingertips weaving
through my hair,
your breath
behind my ear.
When I woke,
I tried to ignore it,
the feeling of your hands.
When I saw them
working in real time,
hot sun, dry ground,
my body became electric.
I chose to indulge
my mind and why,
oh god, it feels good
to feel again.

Your Breath Behind My Ear

My mind is a vine
tangled deep
in the shade.
Thoughts climb
around you
twisting,
nature's force,
unresisting.

Nature of Attraction

How to tame a woman:

by the hands of a man
who owns his strength,
whose love is a force
known through fingertips,
spine and gaze.
See me, touch me.

His presence is power.

His Presence Is Power

I hid in your love,
until I crawled out
from under your arm
and found who I am.

I am nothing like I thought.

I am wild and fearless,
mysterious, goddess.

Want me this way,
speak to her—
the woman with eyes ablaze,
breath thick with passion,
body tearing to feel,
mind tangled,
spirit of sun,
moon and stars.
I want to be
wanted this way—
in untamed loving.

Do not need me.
Can you be brave?

Growing Out of Codependency

I call you out,
My love, my love,
show me your bones!
Fractured and whole,
I need to see the inside,
flesh and beating.

Show Me Your Bones

Sometimes it happens—
first time meeting
through metal fence wire
tangled in early season
sweet pea vines and you
were a home.
It's not that we grew
to become that,
there is history and time
we haven't shared
but it is the air you bring
and how easily I wrap
my arms around you,
I love you on my lips
as you walk through the door.

You Are A Home

I swallow the breeze,
this is the way to live and die—
drunk on apple blossoms
and sweet grass,
lying in the arms
of a lover.

Spring Fever

You know that feeling,
eyes closed,
all black and red
movements of light,
a universe of blindness,
while hands of afternoon
wind caress your cheek
and lips, skin like velvet,
brushing feathery strands
of hair around the edges of your face
in and out of its fingers.
Sun touches the nape of your neck
and down, kissing ridgelines
of your shoulders,
warmth radiating through
spine and muscle, making way
deep into you.

You know that feeling.

Eyes open, sun set
west-facing sky fades
lavender to peach
to pink and the way
the evening breeze bursts
through the kitchen
and swallows you
standing still in the center
of earth moving, unable to move,
unable to breathe,
until you do, and deeply—
when you know right then
you are entranced and alive,
quieted and untroubled.

You know that feeling.

To be nature's muse,
her lover, the one who hears
her name whispered through air
while trees dance and sky paints,
moon rises full from the east,
water laps and rushes and spills
and *this is all for me.*

You know that feeling.

Nature's Muse

She cries,
I cannot wipe her tears.
I kneel down, folding my body
upon the ground, face pressed
into pine and mullein,
palms flat on grass.
Saltwater streams
as my heart's fire slows
its flame
into a steadier
burn.

We forget how loved we are.

The wind rushes through cedar boughs
and sweeps my cheek
as I raise my head, tears dry.
Acceptance rains,
the sky opens,
and the child's eyes can see.
Her mouth speaks in tongues
as she lifts up her body,
soft in nakedness.
Walls tremble and fall.
A wild rose opens
in the spring sun.

Inner Child

What if we made a place
within a place that exists,
in the cool of riverside green
and heat of summer fields,
where we walked and talked
and worked and loved
to birdsong and howling winds,
slept under star-strewn sky
and woke to low morning fog
stepping out of bed bare toed
onto dew-damp grass—

what if we ate slow-growing food
knowing names of every seed
of every bean and grain
set to plate before us,
flowers filling vases
spilling every spectrum hue
and we could see and taste
and touch and know
the very minutes that it takes
to make a life and to be alive—

what if we shared it all,
inviting loved ones and strangers,
creating spaces, making homes
and neighbors with those who want to be
part of a greater family,
fostering care for handmade labor,
ceramics and paints,
florals and vegetables,
heart-filled speech in word and rhyme,
poetry spoken and lyrics tuned to

instrumental accompaniments
strummed in strings and pounded keys—

what if we lived our years
learning how to be full and free,
striving for the riches of meaning
and joy in simplicity,
making history—
what if we taught others
how to do it too—

what if we made this place
within a place that exists?

Heaven On Earth

Dissolving,
absorbed in the river of life,
I become water.
We were made to move
and wind our way through rock
to the open sea.
Hands open and releasing,
let go, breathe,
let it carry you,
diving into the deep
of the cool pool
to find its current.
We were not made
to hold on,
feet in the mud bank
clinging to the vines.

Be Like Water

My heart
swells,
contracts,
I feel
I cannot
bear it,
and I do.
I laugh
and weep,
holding
the balance
of all things
within me.

33

A full moon in Libra
rose with the equinox,
an introduction
to the beating heart
of our budding bough
due to bloom
in seven months.
It's light descended
and settled,
illuminating circles,
whispering promises,
leading me toward
something new
that has always been.
Looking into
my womb that day,
a thin gold band
placed in my hand,
grandmother's ring,
an eternal symbol.
I sat with sister
and mother,
cards stacked,
turned its face,
a circle of blue
holding a smaller circle,
sea serpent spirit,
second chakra,
deep in the pelvic bowl.

Oh, divine mother,
center of desire,
home in her own,
wrapping herself around us

in waters of emotion,
gestures of protection,
express your nature,
she says.
I see your form,
circles carrying circles
within my body.
All is one.

Libra Moon

Carousels of swallowtails
float around me where I sit
in green outside the room
where you lay dying.
My belly swollen with new life,
this gift and repossession
is both my fragility
and my strength.
These fluttering wings,
delicate things,
I hear from somewhere,
Disarm! Find your softness,
I try so hard to hold on.

Swallowtails

Mama–
I say it like a breath
and a prayer.
The moon rose full
over me and I thought
of your stainless heart,
I could see it.
Your arms—
my eyes were closed.
I slept and you told me
you were here,
with me.
You held me.
My eyes—
your arms around
my arms around
my baby girl
and I woke up,
my eyes open
to the invisible weight
of your embrace.
You held me, here.
Don't go—
I'll close my eyes again,
don't go.
Stay, while I sleep
a little longer—

Your Arms Around My Arms

Fear's fire set
close to home,
as it burns
do I run?

I am a tree,
feet flat on ground,
skin, blood, and bone
sink into earth,
roots grow,
reach darkness
twist, breathe, drink.
Straighten my spine,
I lift up my arms!
Palms open to light,
absorb air,
sun, heat, moisture.
Face tilted toward sky,
I am made of soil,
water, and light.
Part my lips,
tongue makes sounds
in whispers, heart opens,
slow, steady beats.
I sing, eyes close.
I am a tree,
I do not run or hide.
Daughter's hand
brushes my cheek,
son's laugher
spills over me
as he climbs,

arms around my neck.
I am rooted and living,
covering what grows beneath me.

I Am A Tree

Purveyor of softness, she said.
Her words keep coming to mind.
When the world turns
in sorrow and suffering,
I will follow the call into the meadow,
into forests, into fields,
I will lay my head on a peony bloom
and say, *you can too.*

Softness

Sky strewn with pink
I call the western lights,
ethereal form, pearlescent neon.
Before this last glow on a hilltop,
I lay my fears to the ground.
Prayers move from my tongue
to wind, carrying over
distant pines finding flight
to the heavens on the wings
of a rising moon, full and heavy
at my back—surrendered.
Is this what the moon
has been asking of me?
Following it through clouds
in the east of late afternoons
and through nights, each day
revealing more light,
but tonight
in the reflection of its fullness,
I feel the weight of my presence.
It is time to release, another birth
making room in this holy body.
It is space that I crave now,
contractions for the emptiness,
to walk fields toward an endlessly
stretching horizon, expanse.
Do you feel this? This is transition.
What needs to flow?
The void of the womb
will give room for
something brand new.

Transition

The sun rose
from behind clouds
of winter's end
and snowflakes fell
stars of white
from your sky.
The mourning dove
sang until noon
your favorite song.
I cut the first bucket
full of tulips, long stems,
bunches of amethyst buds,
and as their ruffled petals
slowly opened,
I heard your voice say
purple is your favorite color.

Purple Tulips

Wild grass sparkles,
dew from night's rain,
up the hill,
through the field,
middle of June
feels like the day
I lost you.
Under oak arms,
hands on moss
sliding down against
its trunk seeping
with moisture
resting body
into bark skin.
Sun-lit trees,
clouds sweeping
cool and wet,
barely summer,
weaving flowers
together in a vase
morning wind,
open doors,
last September.
Heart aches,
alone with memory,
ashes in my hand.
Hiding in leaves,
bird chatter,
water droplets
fall slow
leaf to leaf.
Green forest edge,
fog-strewn mountains

yellow finches burst
like paint splashes,
weeping,
feeling so close
to the depth of it all.
Pine branches
arched in a heart,
water-soaked wild
nature meeting me,
drinking sweet medicine,
swallowing dark
soil-turned mulch
and mushrooms
fill me,
nursing my pain
until I sigh.
Small white feather
floats down,
press my cheek
to tree savoring
softness and green.
Fingers dig into layers,
folding myself into
billowy pillows
of seasoned ground,
it is not enough
to be above
wanting to be
buried,
covered by love.
More white feathers.
Dogs bark,
car engine fires,

voices echo,
sunlight shifts
birds in flight,
she gives final words
in whispers,
There is
so much
joy ahead.
Getting up,
moving on,
standing still
looking toward
my path,
white feather drifts
and lands creating
a triangle of three.
Walk to the height
of the hill facing
a westward valley,
palms open,
her body carrying
on a breeze
settling over
wildflowers,
her spirit alive,
dancing circles
around me
with the wind.

White Feathers

Found the flowers
well above my head,
abundant pollinator feast.
Bumblebee asleep
in a lavender hug,
hummingbird indulgently dips
in gladiolus pools,
swallowtail butterfly lands
on a bunch as I thread
a few more strands in my hand,
darling little human creatures,
low to the ground, children
of the earth running naked
under overflowing blossoms
tasting bits of this and that,
throwing petals in the air
sometimes holding hands,
sometimes digging-in-dirt hands,
always buzzing, making movement
and this dance together is the finest.

Pollinator Feast

Taste fruit,
hear water drip.
See wind move
everything around you.
Smell the sweetness
of a flower,
touch the skin
of your body.
This is life.

The Sensual Life

This kiss is pleasure,
soft winds of late morning
in the sun's saturated heat,
Queen Ann's lace umbel heads
subtly sway
as leaves of cottonwoods
shiver and shake
like sequins in the sun.
A red-headed woodpecker soars
between three pines,
white circles on black,
art on his wings.

Calls My Love Like the Mourning Dove

Smoke circles
dance with light streams
through long windows
set into the arched
roof of the cabin.
At the foot of stairs,
I hold an abalone shell
and bundled leaves of sage.

For Charles, I say.

I imagine this
was his favorite place
in the house—
A-framed pitch
tilts a westward window
and the eyes cannot help
looking up and out
at the low sun
preparing descent
into the horizon
of the Pacific.
Only swaying lines
of forest separate
views of the ocean,
where I stand
everything is golden.
With each wave
of my hand
and billow of white,
I lean into
the discomfort,
and say,
thank you.

From his desk
where he passed
last spring,
I speak to him
through the mysterious
alternate of time,
it is not an easy thing,
holding layers of feeling
with every object I see.

My son hollers
from outside,
he has hidden
a collection
of shells found
in a wire basket.
I walk toward
rhododendrons
taller than I am,
a clam is tucked
between the arch
of two branches.
Under a canopy
of cedars, I find
another shell
and I exclaim,
knees in moss
and cones
and fir needles.

We pick morning
glory blooms
and salal berries,

fashioning little ladies
with foraged fuchsia's,
white-petaled skirts,
strawberry leaf hats,
crowns of privet flowers.
Using grass blades
for string we smile
at each other
with every creation.

Salty sweet
green air mixes
with understanding
and I breathe.
I am learning about
the uncomfortable—
it is okay to be in it,
we do not have to
run from it.
We can feel
it deeply,
know it is
with us,
and we can
still play and love
and give thanks
for what is,
even in the
presence of loss.

For Charles

Back pressed against
dry grass, spine straight,
arms at my side, palms down.
Eyes closed and breathing,
I feel it all—the weight of myself,
the weight of earth under me,
the weightlessness of wind,
skin drenched in summer's heat,
heat pumping through me in
pathways while I watch colors
through eyelids change from
deep red to orange until I imagine
I am underwater with my eyes open,
a hazy green and blue brightening
as I swim toward the surface.
Right hand on my belly, left on
my heart, words form aloud,
Help me.
I need clarity, to sift through
the deep and find my lifeforce again.
Awaken me.
Opening my eyes, I lift my body—
I am lighter, gentler, and I feel
the tinder spark with a burning
promise of a flame.

I Do the First Right Thing

Fingers in damp soil washed by wet clover,
golden cottonwood leaves glide to the ground.
A towhee swoops into cypress, hazelnut husks
under my feet. Buzz by my ear, the hummingbird
lands on a branch, drying its feathered body
and zooms away.

Your banner over me is love.
You brought me to the banqueting table,
Your banner over me is love.

Grapevine heavy with fruit and green,
kneeling at the woodland's edge,
moss spongy and sword ferns bounce
under the drip of water drops.

You are the vine and we are the branches.
Your banner over me is love.

Standing before a line of redwoods,
water rains from the sky
and beads down my skin,
I lift my head toward the spill.
Fermenting fruit, minerals musty and rich,
the air becomes a lake of lapping abundance.

Lake of Abundance

A full moon swimming in Pisces
gleaming like a glacier
in a dusty rose sea.
Standing on sequoia roots,
under its canopy of arching green,
I watch the planet appear to sink
slowly into distant layers,
its last orbed light bowing
into the ocean's body
before it disappears.

How magnificent to witness
waking at dawn after
the last night of summer,
two years prior—
she removed her physical robe
for her garment of divinity.
I am a Pisces queen
receiving messages from
my Piscean mother
on this holy day,
her spirit boundlessly moves
through the heavens and the earth.
She says,
Listen my sweet angel,
release every want
for anything other
then what is.
Sink deep
into the acceptance
of what is now.
Be here,
only here.

I listen,
and submerge myself
over and over into
the depths of now,
baptizing myself in light.

Full Moon In Pisces

A full moon rises,
I am undressing for the occasion,
removing layers that keep my body
hiding from illumination,
I need to see this,
I need to feel this.

It hurts, it hurts.

Is it enough to make me look,
to sit and cry, rip off the old
cloth and hold it in the light?
From where does this pain flow
and how far into myself does it run?

I kneel to mossy ground,
hawthorn berries red and wet
sink deeper into soil,
apples turning sides into
matter unrecognizable.
This land to which my heart is tied—
home, a geography of earth and body,
here on the map is where I stand,
but how did I get here?
My grandmother's raven hair,
her dark eyes, and I imagine
what courses through my blood,
the unknown I hold,
feeling it in my fingertips,
I see it in dreams,
I hear echoes in the wind.
Thirty-four years I have lived
walking these trails claimed

by gold and blood in the name of god,
stolen land by hands stained red
and this pain seeps from my skin
as the ground thirsts and fires rage.
The more I know myself,
the further back it takes me,
asking that I know what came
before me.

This time is poignant, a reminder
of nature's cycles, creating balance
through seasons of water and fire.
What is being done has been done before
and is my pain part of this cyclical process?

Can we heal what ails us?

Standing naked in the white moonlight,
a force fills darkness
and brings renewal from the depths of death.

My Grandmother's Raven Hair

Barred owl
at woodland's edge,
first morning light.
I cannot break my gaze,
magnificent, eyes circled
in black, head turning
and tilting, feathers
etched in brown and white.

The maples and oaks
have dropped their leaves,
gold for next year's
flower beds. I rake with
enthusiasm and reach
my hand to touch the
mossy trunks of these trees
and say, *thank you*.

Every day I learn one more
reason to exist within
diverse habitats.
A small corridor bordered
by city, woven in green
and river water holds
immensity to teach.
Sustainable life force
pulsing energy to feed,
nourish and heal beneath
my feet, growing up
and around me.
Presence alive, moving
and connecting, comforting
as I look into eyes of wild

animals passing by.
Magic in the way winds
dance around the land,
colors of each season
burst like brushstrokes
up from the soil.
I witness these rich
mysteries and recognize
parts of myself—
I am tied to abide
among the diversity
of the living.

Entangled in ecosystems
of plants and soaring fowl,
a slow awakening,
a remembering of what
I am that I had long
ago forgotten,
before centuries of sleep
covered my eyes.

I want everyone to have
a place tangled in trees
and vines, fields of seed
heads in autumn to inhabit.

Centuries of Sleep

Have you seen
the underside
of a flicker's wing?
The purple cap
of a russula mushroom?
Early winter sun
backlights moss-covered
branches glowing green
and finches cover
brown seed stocks
of wild lemon balm.
I speak prayers,

Our father,
holy is your name,
Your kingdom come,
on earth as it is
in heaven.

You lead me beside still waters,
You restore my soul—

Just as last leaves fall,
tips of limbs
bud and soften,
ready and waiting to open—
and this is how
I will move through the dark—
holding in my hand
what contains light.

My daughter's eyes
are the color of sequoia bark,
my son's,
cornflowers in autumn gold.

Light my path.

The sky is cool blue,
sheaves of ice in the field
melt from grass blades
down into clover
as shadows move with hours.

Illuminate me.

I hear my grandmother's
voice amidst thoughts
as I harvest newly sprouting cleavers
from layers of bark mulch.
Fuzzy leaves sour the tongue,
and a jay as bright as cobalt
stark against woodland edges
cuts through my view.

I am light.

Light In the Dark

I take off my slippers
just to feel the floor,
hurting from separation,
bearing the distance,
feet relax onto boards
creaking like old bones.
I am touching trees
in some way.
My body is begging
to be closer
to what it belongs to.

Grounding

Longing to be
swept away
while belonging
to this present
moment, and this
is what it does—
listening to a song,
making a bouquet,
painting oils
on a canvas,
writing a poem,
having a conversation,
kissing a lover,
walking through
the forest,
napping in the sun,
laughing with children,
crying on the floor.

This Is What It Does

A wetland in winter
is a vibrant place,
red twig dogwood
with willow's ochre-
colored airy stems,
umber edges of spirea
leaves and neon green
striped tufted grass.
Pops of cadmium orange
rose hips burst along edges
of cobalt blue water and sky.
Nature is painting.

Painting of a Winter Wetland

Bathe me in water,
bathe me in light.
What else can do
what this does?
Am I the moon,
a jagged edge
of crystal quartz?
I stay so long
in the dark.

Winter Baptismal

What I live for now
is the white arc suspended
in pale-blue morning sky
and fields of icy jewels
glittering in golden streams.
Unknowingly, I stumbled
into these desires without
anticipation of receiving.
The dark fog of stagnancy
wrapped me blind
until shapes of light
appeared after a clearing
in the night.

What I Live for Now

When it snows,
I can hear a bird in flight
and a body of white
still gleams in shadows
under a silver waning moon
with the dark of early morning.

Morning Snow

February snow
waning crescent
yellow finches
dangling jewels
on birch branches
two hummingbirds
river billows
sun's warmth
against cold
mugwort smoke
heat up my spine
visions in the dark
eyes closed.

Today's Love

Fill up
with pleasure
that compels.

I follow her hands
as she shows meridians,
fingers trail ridgelines
and high points
along my head,
down the collarbone,
we both hold our hearts
in unison.

Days before,
I held my tear-struck face
in my palm
and rocked to calm
the crying baby on my back.
I did not know how I could move
out of despair,
but even there,
the body can receive
its grace.
In the warmth of blood
and swaying hips,
I found immense nurturing
and quieted.

You found it,
you allowed yourself
to be in the moment
completely,
you melted into
your embrace.

We can still,
fill up.

I leave her office
to drive the winding
road home in the dark.
The crescent moon
is always in the forefront
of my view.

Therapy

Children,
nature's splendor,
my two,
illuminating dark,
sparkling multicolor.
I want to be like this.

I dreamed I could fly,
it felt like swimming in air,
moving waves of atmosphere,
body in flight
above city lights,
courtyards and parks,
people looking up,
smiling,
graceful fluidity.

You have to believe
you can fly;
it begins with believing.

I woke
with limitless
possibilities.

Is this the true child?
Untethered from burden,
a hope-filled light
shining in the night—
are we stars
of wonder,
stars bright?

We Are Stars

To love
what you love,
allow it.
Remove every layer,
drop it in a heap
at your feet,
stand naked
with your hands
on your beating chest,
and proclaim:

This is my heart!
I own this,
I own this love!

Unabashed,
fervent,
rise with the power
that waits within.
Subtle accusers
have a way
of dragging us out
of the truth that carries
like dream seeds
in the dark
what lives in us.
How many
keep love
from the light?

Let us try
something else now,
let it out.
Hold it up in the cup

of your hands
like an offering
and use your voice
to create a living contract.

I own this heart!

We carry our truth in love.

Hold It Up

Late winter,
I curbed my loneliness
with pink hanging catkins
of hazelnut trees
and the stellar jay's
cobalt body
in flight through gray,
but I still ache
for human company,
to meet me where I sit.
Then you came,
with sun on your body
and soul, and honesty
on your lips, I laughed
again without effort,
feeling myself at home.
When you left,
I kept the warmth
pressed between my chest,
knowing now
our place together,
the space we have built
through time.

Friendship

The first bird call of morning
and my soul jolts awake.
Window open in the dark
of a February freeze.
I can be asleep for days
flipping switches,
closing doors,
pressing buttons
in modern convenience.
Is this why my grandmother
always slept with the window open
beside her bed at night?
Drafty upstairs room
with no heat in winter and
she still kept a couple inches
of the outside coming in.
Did she know the animal in her skin?
Hot blood coursed with life
for the nature it belonged to,
in her farmhouse
no longer surrounded by field or forest
now houses and highways,
she entwined her breath
with that of the earth
through that small crack of a pane.
The candle flickers out
and I am almost glad for it.
Somehow, even the light of fire
feels imposing to this hour
before the sun rises,
and I want to feel the truth
of what really is
without my making.

First Bird Call of Morning,
The Animal In My Skin

I take longer to dress—
for most my life I thought
I was something to hide.
Now, I linger in the softness and shadows
allowing time to touch my body with light.

Naked, Thirty-Six

I want to be touched
with electricity and divinity,
led home to that Holy Wild
only found when we meet.

Heavenly Chemistry

Oh mother,
I hold the redwood tree,
fall on my knees and weep.
How lonely I am
until I'm pressed
into the softness of my pain.
When my body folds,
sinks into the deep—
I lose the separation
and rest within
the stillness of grief.

First Two Weeks of March

March fifteenth, three years
waking up without you,
I wrap your purple
down jacket around me
as I do every day in winter—
I wear your socks
and look for you in everything.
This is what I do: wrap myself up
in signs and connections
to pull you close to me.

I won't let this be
the end of our relationship!

I stir chia seed hearts into
the bubbling pot of oats for breakfast.
Plum blossoms wave and scatter,
morning rain subsides to opening sky,
warm air moves in and a rainbow
arched ahead beams at each side
of the road I drive, while a song
I know plays and I sing quietly,

it is a glorious day
to be born.

On Your Birthday

Plum blossoms fall
like snow on the first day
of spring; on my knees,
I spread my mother's ashes
into soil reciting words of Jesus.
This is my body broken for you,
my blood poured out for you,
I think of her womb holding me,
mine newly empty,
both our bleeding bodies bent
given in communion
with our children.

Spring is the mother
in gestation, holding past
and future together in one seed
developing within her.
All will be born again,
drinking from her breast,
held in the curve of her arm
beside the beating of her chest.

Spring Is My Mother

Last of the cotton floats
on invisible wind currents,
I think of souls on their
ethereal procession into eternity.
I sit here, on the other side
of the glass window.

My grandmother's birthday,
two years of finding her presence
in everything other than
her tangible body.

My mother's whispered secrets,
sometimes through birds,
on the breeze, often in dreams—
I hear their voices sing loudly
in silence and my heart aches
in its fervent dance,
a continual improv of holding on,
then letting go;
it spins, this waking and breathing life,
with visions and dream life.

Placing the morning's blooms
in a ceramic pitcher,
it was Marilyn Mae
who gave me
my earliest memories
of flowers in a vase.

Mary Ellen,
outside with a shovel
in the soil,
hay on her clothes,
dressed in overalls.

My inheritance—
seeds of slow and simple
appreciation,
crossed with passion
and faith.
I listen
for their heavenly voices,
singing through the
sweet pea vines
and I sing back,
mothers,
hold me,
help me still.

You Gave Me Dream Seeds

Son perched in the arms of a cherry tree,
dropping tart red fruit into baskets.
I sit with daisies, daughter tunneling
through blueberries and tangled grapevines.
Last June, I wept in dahlia rows
after watching blackbirds land on cattails,
Where is our home? What do we do?
knowing the depth of my heart's desire,
I was ready to root and grow.
In the quiet bright of mid-morning sun
curled in overgrown edges of the
grassy garden path I heard,
Wait, just a little longer.
Finish what you started here.
There is a surprise ahead,
and it is good.
Words of validity, as if they flowed
from the mouth of my mother
who could see the future
from a dimension unknown to me,
and I believed her.

Monument of Praise

Always walking
a fine line between
dreaming and waking life.
Sometimes I see the future
in my sleep, sometimes
I lose myself in fear.
Last night I dreamt
of hummingbirds
and an old friend;
today I woke to light
and wandered the yard
sunbathed and slow,
observing my daughter.
One foot she walks
by instinct, the other
by learning, a new
stumbling and wondrous
kind of being.
Could unlearning
be the brush that softens
and blends harsh contrasts
between worlds of
mind and spirit?
To live like a
toddling child,
alive and curious—

Mind and Spirit

The first child
came the night
God in me spoke
and lit the dark places
of my mind with
a bright light,
I have a gift for you,
love you have not known,
say yes or no,
do you want it?
A flash appeared in the white
and I saw love,
a shapeless presence,
feeling the existence
of my child before the seed
of him was planted
in my womb,
Yes,
in trembling reverent fear,
Yes.
I clothed myself with trust,
woven pieces around me.
The second, a dream vision,
waking to the sound
of her name on my tongue,
ten years moving in and out
of eternal mysteries until
the unfolding of her fulfillment.
Born a prophecy and a testament,
her warm skin a letter
of hope and divinity.

Makaiah and Adia

How do I hold
love's essence
whose home
are my children?

I am the earth,
body of soil and water.
May my land be
the ground they run to
and press upon,
my voice their flowing
mountain stream,
may my heart's beat
rock them to sleep,
may they abide
in the temple
of my love's essence,
until they recognize
within themselves,
they are home.

For My Children

I stand before
a throne of green,
the threshold brings
me to my knees,
I am sorry, forgive me.
Pardoned under
arms of sequoias.
Stillness hangs,
repentance opens me.
I remember I can trust
Her sovereignty.

Threshold

Pay attention—
after the dark,
it seemed to rise,
the way shining
to what I needed—
water.
I swallow it full,
and with first light
run the tub
and submerge myself
in salt and liquid.
Birds sing,
the sun is coming.
I breathe in,
out,
in,
out,
following meridians
with fingertips,
whispering everything
I need, I have.
I am held.
I am loved.
I am healthy.
I am holy.
Absorbed with minerals
and truth, I rise to walk outside,
ocean waves of wind
roll through the garden
in rushes and recessions,
trees sway like bodies dancing,
arms up in praise for the spirit
that moves them.

Birds with grass-filled beaks
dart and disappear,
the sun lifts its light
higher and further,
I stand still in its stream.

I no longer read books,
those are their stories,
this is mine—

there are days of darkness
when I cannot see myself
or where to move.
Then I cry out
for the sake of this life
I have been given;
a shift happens—
morning comes,
I awaken.

How I Wake Up

Bury my face in grass,
petals brush skin,
I want to surrender
every resistance
and sink my body in
the earth of you.
Maybe I yearn
to be held
by the foundation,
maybe I yearn
to feel the firmament.
I yearn to meld myself into
everything you are,
and be one.

Depths of You

Words cannot make sense
of the weather I feel,
earth always seems
to weep in the midst
of great loss.
She is warm today,
her body wrapped
around mine, face pressed
to the green of her chest,
and I am washed
in the gentleness
of her tears.

The Weather I Feel

A night owl spoke
through the dark
while viral eruptions
within my body
settled into something
less violent.

I called my father
earlier in the day,
only intending to
inform him of illness,
yet I cried my
deepest secret,
I am afraid
I am destined
to live a life
of pain!
A wound-up ball
of fear came loose,
sobs of distrust
carried toward my body
and the fates,
softened the tightness,
I began to soothe
myself as a friend.

Sister body,
thank you
for holding me,
supporting me through,
you are amazing,
how you fight
and care!

I love you,
I am forever grateful
for your loving strength.

Bobbing on gentle ocean
waves, breath a silent
floating device
weightless in salt water,
I rode the tide as it moved,
finding my way through.

Your body is your best friend.

A Night Owl Speaks

The clouds part and I finally accept
what my body has been saying.
I tried to fight all morning,
but here I am spreading myself
between fruit trees like mulch,
rib cage sinking into wild grass,
hips twisted and barefoot.
I undress slowly
as the sun casts out
trembling into radiant heat.
What was I thinking?
Too much—
when was the last time
I watched cotton seed
move through branches,
palms caressing
with blades of green
in the forefront of view?
Too long—
since youth,
or childhood,
before love became
sacrifice and to-do lists.
This view reminds me
of my first sweetheart,
and it feels like
coming home.
I don't want to
leave you,
I want to stay,
here—

When Clouds Part

I am drawn to tunnels of nature,
arching, twisting,
encompassing places
that pull me,
swallow me.
Not the solid body of a cave
or belly of a mountain,
but softer bending lines
and walls of dappled light.
No, rock won't do.
I need earth and water,
the way they meet together,
swaying and quivering
while wind breathes through them.
I know the ancient cavern
moves slowly over time
in a particular way
that I just can't see,
but I see this—
how you blend light and dark,
catching strands
of my hair with wild rose vines,
the way plum blossoms
drift to my lips and stick,
demanding I taste them.
I have a path out—
after all,
I am in a tunnel of trees.
What I want is no way out,
just soft ground
to lay my head
and time.

Tunnel of Trees

A hummingbird drinks
from dangling purple
comfrey blooms and flits
over to the azaleas,
while the tiger swallowtail
lands on a sun-drenched leaf
of Indian plum and stays a while.
Bees hum somewhere within
trumpet cups of rhododendrons,
pink flowers fall
like skirts to the ground.
The squirrel does what it does,
scratching and jumping distances
along branches of redwoods,
a robin lands on a perch
of the pea trellis
with a nut in its mouth.
All of these do what they do
and I wonder—
what is it
that we do?

What We Do

The spider's silken thread
attached to my chair,
arcs to meet dandelion heads,
zigzagging and moving light rays
with the first morning sun
on this first summer's day.
I didn't see it at first—
waving like a laundry line,
but I moved slightly so
as the earth moved with me
and I caught that golden shimmer
in my sight.

For years I did not see.

At the front of our house
holes in the pavement
fill with rain and men complain,
that we should fix it—
I watch robins land,
dipping their brown heads
and orange bellies
in and up and out,
feathers ruffled in the water,
and my daughter delights
as her boots trudge through,
splashing as cars do.

For years I did not see
how the hair like strands
are always here,
connected and weaving
through our surroundings,

nearly invisible
without sitting yourself
in the right light
at the right time
and opening your eyes.

Nothing here needs fixing.

A Spider's Silken Web

Like fine wine,
we bide our time
in years,

something is happening—
you are not the same
as you were then,
you will not be
who you are today,

and I want that
swirl of complexity
and the depth of you
lingering at the finish.

I will wait.
It will be worth it—
your fullness
poured out into my hands,
and I'll raise my glass to you
and drink.

Aging

Edge of a doorway,
I am in the shadows,
tile and metal,
he is center
in a room of gray
and he dances,
changing clothes
wildly thrown to the side,
dressing up in new robes,
I cannot take my eyes
off him.
Trancelike force
magnetized,
pulled face to face
our bodies pressed,
aligned before each other,
electric energy,
rhythmic precision,
completely absorbed by
presence within,
fully in my body,
moving as one.
Lips open silently
singing words
with intention,
whispers of lyrics flow
from depths of my being,
power pours through
this quietness
with a quality
that feels like honey
dripping from my mouth.

Honey, Aquarius Full Moon

Green is the color
of my heart;
I water gardens
with my tears.
Giver and receiver,
I am both love
and lover.

Who Can Hold My Longing?

Deep and wide
is the dark water—
I am learning
how to swim.
What choice do
I have? Drown
now or try to
cut through
the weight of
this ocean?

From the death
of one comes
multitudes of
little deaths.
This is the water
I speak of.

I am the crater,
a vast hole
excavated, gaping
and expansive.
When it rains,
waves form,
churning, growing.

I thought I knew
myself until she left—
our family ground
cracked, I watched
it fall from a distance.
I cannot return
to where I was.

From One Death Comes Multitudes

To know myself?
I am infinite!
The further I explore
the dark mystery within,
I realize the universe
I am.

Immeasurable

Do you
love Jesus?"
He asks.
Most assuredly,
"Yes!"
Everything in me
responds to the
perfect symmetry
of his being,
I crave holy masculinity,
long to dwell in
divine femininity,
I desire a man who can
sit in the depths
of communion.
Show me
the God in you!
I want to know
the God in you!

Show Me the God In You

I don't know why
the beauty strikes me so
in just an arm's reach
for a purple plum
in dappled morning light.
This pear-picking, Queen Ann's
lace-wading life looking up
from the inside of a tree heavy
with ripening fruit, tiptoed
and stretching to grasp it
is as good as the dripping
sweetness of it.
I am filled with abundance.
I must be made for this.

Queen Ann's Lace Wading Life

On my knees
in the yarrow,
a dragonfly lands
on my shoulder.
You know my heart aches?
Black and blue
wings hold still—
two paused and present,
open and receiving
each other.
I speak to you,
you stay,
and say to me,
this is grace.

Dragonfly

Abalone shell sky
with a wisp of arced light
curved before my eyes,
when just a moment before
everyone else's needs
kept me indoors.
I almost didn't leave
unapologetically, forcefully
for myself this was
a last minutes dash
to openness and exhalation.
Here I am, barefoot
on roots, stopped
in my tracks looking
out at sundown—
seeing arms wave me in
to embrace this
loving place,
this for-me space,
I smile and sigh,
I am held high
under the new moon's
slivering eye and wings
of a great bird form
in pink neon above me,
exaltation.

Exaltation

Kissed by summer wind,
she whispered in my ear,
honey, it's almost time,
get ready.
I waited for the rising fear
to take me from her air,
but I felt anticipation
in waiting
for the coming
of my love.

On Your Way To Me

She calls,
I sink deep
in the dark,
breech within
the womb
of red clay.
Deeper, heavier,
embodied by
a cavern,
my body sitting
below
the earth's surface.
Energy drops
fast and low
into my pelvic bowl.
She calls,
I feel gravity's pull
force me further
into darkness.

Don't Be Afraid

I resist—
fearing the dark
even after all this time.
I did not know how I fought,
how I ran,
until she pulled my body
down, so fast, so heavy,
into the depths of some
unknown space, my heart
racing and I thought,
don't take me.
Don't take me.
I am afraid,
of what I cannot know
in the light.

Surrender Takes a Unique Strength

In her room, at her bed,
the summer of her death,
she apologized.
This was the first time,
the circle's final lapse
looking back, she could
understood her pain.

She explains,
I did not know how
to go through the grief;
your father worked hard
but was not there,
I was alone.

Mother, I was sixteen,
you were forty-five,
brothers and sister
still so little while I
changed the pump
draining blood from
your severed chest,
you wept,
hair coming out
in fistfuls
when your father died.

Could we know
how to go through
this grief?

When I was five,
my golden lab went missing.
For days I called for her,

Angel, Angel,
up and down
country roads, only to find
her dismembered by a
freight truck on the highway.

Cousin Janice died
on my birthday,
killed by a semi
on the interstate.
I remember crying,
somehow feeling
the heaviness was tied
to my right to be alive,
and I carried it all this time.

How could I know?

Whitest fur,
one eye brown,
one eye green,
tiny kitten
following me to the truck.
I told him not to leave—
asked him to help bring
her back to the house.
Daddy, please,
she might be
underneath—
late for church,
she'll move,
it will be fine,
don't worry.

How could I know
not to bury all grief
inside myself?
My body believed
it couldn't trust a man,
the way he holds the wheel,
driving full speed,
heavy-handed power,
without pause to listen
and consider
what she feels—

when she feels
everything,
and he leaves,
hard worker,
good provider,
means no harm,
she is alone
in her grief.

Thirty years since
I first met death,
and find myself
knowing now
what my mother knew.

What I Know Now

Rose hips are turning
their orange bodies
to a red sheen,
while a stellar jay's
blue wings dart
to a fruitless tree.
An apple falls
to the ground;
I hold three purple
plums in my hand
and see so much
I cannot contain—
waves of sustaining
lifeforms ripening,
it is harvest, where
is my basket? I left
it for a moment of
unintentional pace—
a walk without task;
days are busy going
and doing, demanding
and fixing, while so much
richness spoils at our feet.
Yet this, is the miracle
of what is living,
nothing is wasted,
always recreated.

Looking up toward a sky
of pearlescent light,
a hummingbird stops
in mid-flight, body like
a cross erected on a
mount of air.

This is where it is—
what we are waiting for,
the deeper longing,
the unmet desire we keep
tracing around at the edges.
Go inside this circle,
put yourself in the midst.
This is where we meet
our absence and our filling.

This Is Where We Meet

My father tells me
he wants me
to be whole,
and I think,
I am whole—
I just don't feel it.

Spirit speaks,
I am here,
not to heal
your diseases
or your longing,
I am here
to heal *you.*

You are the water
and rock from
which it flows,
undam that mighty
force and wash
the residual scum
off your riverbed.

What you search for
is nothing, what you
contain is everything.

Open the door,
turn on the light,
I am here,
this is salvation.

Wholeness

Silver strands
catch like moonlight
across dark water,
who am I
trying to please,
but myself?
I keep going
back and forth—
should I cover
this nature?
But today,
in this light,
I see
the shimmering
length of its allure,
and I allow it
to be as it is.

Going Gray

She took me down,
brought me to my
roots and buried me,
broke the dammed-up
places and released
a rushing river.
Now the spark,
fan the flame in waiting
for heat to rise like wings,
burn back down
and carry me.

I Dreamt of Yellow

I found myself
in a field of flowers,
back pressed to
thirsty earth watching
bees move around me,
on most days.
It is okay to be
deeply lonely;
because I am here,
and it takes time,
unwavering attention
to know her.
It is okay to move slow
and love myself.

Summer 2022

Fruit hangs heavy and ripe,
what we have missed
decomposes at our feet.
By now, I know the cycle,
death comes in September.
There is no comfort in this
repetition; some seem
to be untouched by the
harvest blade, yet they
too will one day know
the season they are in.
Today, a friend lost
her baby, there are no
words for this grieving.
I write to release what I
cannot hold, the unknowable,
the cyclical, the mystery of
death's transfer.
Nature's way is abundance
and regeneration through the
damp dark decay of what we
taste in the lighter season.
This is not the end,
but a continual exchange.

The Harvest

A creation story
tells of a life once
lived in a garden,
walking with God
in the cool of evening,
naked and wholly unified.

What is this filthy cloth
I wear? Why am I hiding?

He wants more—
to know the heights
of sovereignty without
recognizing authority
in his nakedness.

Why do I cover my love
with lies?

He reaches for power
and eats it, binding
himself to fate.

Shame is the separation,
the tear between humanness
and divinity—his unity.
Here, he cannot live within
the abundance of his earth;
here, he has to prove his worth
through labor, and murder.

This is our story—

A birthright was sold
for a bowl of stew,

when we could have
had the entire land
in our name.

Garments unravel slowly
at my feet, what I have
worn through generations,
I will not keep,
the more skin
I see brings a
forgotten reality,
that we are beings.

I was not born to plow
fields endlessly and
starve from the lack.

Garden of Eden, Our Birthright

First of October,
I'll take out the dog—
code for let me grab
a little whisky and sneak
outside with the last light,
watch hummingbirds speed
through tops of cottonwood trees,
this is where I will be,
with the bats in a drunken flight,
stunned by the moon appearing
at my right from behind
the great sequoia. Is this real?
All this color of daylight
fading into night, witnessing
the waking of life—
bullfrogs and crickets, sky
a dusky peach, silhouettes
of conifers dancing in the finale
of this season's evening heat.
If you want the sound
of a babbling brook
or a rushing river in your yard
when you have neither—
plant a cottonwood.
The birds are nesting
somewhere behind me
in thick redwood arms,
occasionally they zip
over my head, two of them
in play, energy in motion—
I was not taught to believe in
the wholeness of existence.
If *this* is real, what about

my dreams at night,
the heart pulling threads
I feel tugging my body
to unknown spaces and time?

The light in me
wants the light in you,
the light in me
wants the light in you,
the light in me
wants the light in you.

First of October

As a child
I hid in meadow grass
and daisies,
alone but not lonely,
grasshoppers for company
and the black oak.
I knew the arms
of the pine
would hold me.
I want this for you—
your unforgotten nature,
waking up to remember
sleeping with starlight
above our eyes
and pond water baths.
This is where we belong,
you and I.

Pond Water Baths

I looked into
the grasshopper's eyes,
watched its belly
rise and fall with breath.
We share this air,
I am finding
miracles everywhere.

On the Head of a Dahlia Flower

Sun-drenched throw across the bed,
I am unfurled trying to catch
every inch of light into my woven fibers.
Someone hold me,
wrap me around your body
while glitter streams of dust float by.

Heat Blanket

Sword ferns bounce under
a seemingly invisible force,
until the spotted towhee appears
moving to skeleton stems
of rose campion, finding
what seeds remain.
It is early autumn, the morning
light is clear and bright after
last night's rain as it rises
through layers of tree lines
and twisting branches
and sparkling grasses,
dusting the chair where I sit.
I know I am not the only one
to observe this glory,
the garden spider's orbed life's work,
her art strewn between the trunks
of two redwoods backlit, golden.
A gray squirrel cautiously visits
the front porch, finds a nut
and darts away.
I want to be the sanctuary,
a living place open without refuse.
Plants and animals are easy to love,
loving myself is a practice.
And you, the face that mirrors mine,
my continual challenger—
you who holds the flame
under my eyes revealing what lies
just beyond the illusion of my darkness—
I want to be your temple too,

spacious and bright,
reflecting your light.
This is the home I am becoming.

The Home I Am Becoming

Honey,
I am sorry
for your hurt,
you deserve the
love you long for.
I am here to
hold all of you,
release expectation,
offer your desire,
but do not
give up, patience is
nature's way.
Allow time to work
behind the scenes,
believe in what
you cannot see.
You know now you
can no longer fight;
when you feel
the deep wounds,
when you feel
the disappointment,
when you feel
rejection and the
rising heat of
resentment, breathe.
Breathe it in
and breathe it out,
pause, and love yourself.
Find the calm within
and soothe your
body back to remembrance,
you are infinitely loved.

Allow yourself this,
touch it to your lips,
taste it on your tongue,
swallow it until
your belly is full,
write it over your heart,
wrap it around your arm,
place it on the soles of your feet,
until you are enfolded
within the love garment
of your very being.

From the Mouth of Self Compassion

Everyday sackcloth and ashes,
shaving my head in my mind,
I said I wanted home,
that is what I am becoming.
I said I wanted intimacy,
takes a dissolving,
the depth of knowing.
Here in silence, within stillness,
surrendered body to darkness,
I meet *you.*

You say,
abundance is here,
from the ground
everything grows.

In My Dying

She speaks, *turtle medicine.*
A year ago, I watched
a full moon rise from the east,
sky icy blue and dusted pink,
its hollows and craters
momentous in my eyes,
be in your power,
do not be afraid
of what you carry,
she whispers like wind
through canyons
of my mind; she was right,
a slow transforming of light.
I am aglow and eclipsed
pressed by my earth body
and the space between.
Slowly, you move,
shadows will absolve,
your reflection spells of truth,
you are interwoven and free.

Blood Moon

Maybe it begins here—
hands outstretched
touching trees,
eyes locked intent
on seeing pathways
in bark skin.
I thought I could look
a stranger in the eye
without wavering;
I was wrong.
My body fought it,
mind compulsive—
how long has it been
since I gazed into the
soul of someone,
touched my palm to
their crown saying,
beloved, sister, friend—
with only a gesture
of presence like looking?
What did I find trying
to see her?
I found I am still blind,
wanting to be healed.

Women's Circle

My heart keeps splitting open,
this is good—
a stone-cold wall doesn't love,
and these cracks
in the tender places
fracture the bones of my lies.
Each time I can see deeper,
feel more, and I want
to pour it out upon you,
this healing that rises
from the inside.

Heart Break

I have found a lover
in the arms of nature,
held with affection
by sun and moon
in rain-drenched fields—
yet I long to meet
the wild man who takes
my hand and subdues me
into his earth.
Where is the one who moves
and breathes like wind,
feels like fire and stands firm
like a deep-rooted tree?
Where is the one who
pours out like water
and carves his way through rock?
I want to know your turning,
how the moon pulls you toward me.
I will wait laid upon the belly
of this valley, listening
to love songs from birds' mouths,
calling for the mountain you are
to find me in your sight.

Wild Man

I howl to the moon,
this is the way I cry
my freedom,
this is my dance
untethered and wild,
I am sovereign
and light
before the dark
my crescent
arc appears
and I sing,
I am free,
I am free,
I am free.

Howl To the Moon

I will not wash the
gold dust from my face,
I drink from a sacred cup,
dancing in robes of royal blue
singing
moon sister, moon sister,
to this fullness.
Inscribed is a letter
sealed by fire
held in the palm
of my hand,
my blood and breath
a passageway into
new lands I rule.

Robes of Royal Blue

Full circle
weaving webs
under an iridescent snow moon.
Hearts are hearths
we share our flames
breathing heat into
the night.
Visions pressed
into chests burning,
in this light
we see one
in another.

Full Moon in Leo

Buttons through slits
loosen my blouse,
fingers weave around
my skirt waist,
pull at the hems,
undress me,
I want to reveal
myself to you.
I have stood naked
too many times
before a man
in waiting when
I thought this was
being known;
now I know
I want your hands
on me, delicately
focused and intently
desirous to discover
every hidden place
slowly in time,
noticing the way
cloth falls down
around my skin
until you can see
my naked heart
beating through
my chest.

Undress Me Until You See Me

Wake me up!
This is what you do
when your eyes open
and I can feel the sun in them.

Wake Me Up

In the hospital
you held my hand and said,
You're going to have a daughter,
I smiled, doubted,
focused on first rounds
of chemo through your veins.
Your lives paralleled through time
nine months of heart beats and monitors,
my womb grew, yours died,
I could taste the poison
and my blood mix,
a sacred flight of angels
in our midst
this year of my life—
thirty-three,
your room number,
the time of your final breath,
and all of this dancing
between dimensions
like a river of watery spirit
moving through caverns,
I weep
for what I lost
and what I received.

Nine Months

Body on stone,
hair caught in a blackberry vine,
eyes closed sun soaked
at the river's side.
This is intimate,
this is soft,
this part of me that flows
from the mouth of rock.
Who can meet me here
to taste this holy water?
It is a winding way
up current to find
the source but it is pure
and the sun is shining,
kneeling down, hands cupped,
I drink this water alone.

Drink This Water

Do you know where to find the wild things?
In the bramble at the edges
of field and forest,
blackberry vine draped over fences
where little cottonwood suckers
weave with hazelnut trees
and the dried seed heads
of last season browned out.
This is where life is,
hidden in the thicket.
The wren stood its perch
singing and singing,
calling in the morning
and I want this unkempt mess,
I am it.
When I knew this
I could no longer
choose sod under my feet.
Seeing the truth of our nature
holds more value
than comfort.

Edges and Borders

She touched me
and she spoke,
You are light.
My naked body
refracted into
pieces of color,
rainbow prisms
arching from my skin.

Light Worker

I was planted in the earth
of my mother's womb,
grown within a universe
of dark and light.
She was my first sun
and ocean water,
bones and riverways,
mountainous landscapes,
her breath, my air
and every year
when the ground
is ice and daffodils rise,
I cannot separate myself
from my first home.
I hold in my hands
ashes of her body.
Is this all that is left?
Then she speaks
in the silence,
I see her face
in my mind
she says,
Honey, I am here.
I am with you now.
Let's do this together today.
She sings to me through
waves of frequencies,
My angel, I still hold you,
I sit in mudra,
shawl around my head,
she pours water light
glistening with stars,
bursting from my crown

like a spring from the rock.
Ong Namo, we say,
Satnam vibrating
from my tongue,
I can see the divine.

February 26th

ABOUT THE AUTHOR

Hannah King is an Oregon native, born at the feet of the Siskiyou Mountains. Raised on river water, wild grass and oak savanna, exploring the rural environments of home was her childhood nurturing. She carries the blood of indigenous ancestors, flower farmers, horticulturists, writers, teachers, landscape painters, and these threads are expressed through her writings, art and daily work out in the flower fields. She moved north in her twenties to fertile Willamette Valley and fell in love with the expansive views, meandering waterways and lush coast range. She is rooted in Corvallis, Oregon.

We Are Wanderers is her first published book of poetry.

www.ingramcontent.com/pod-product-compliance
Lightning Source LLC
Chambersburg PA
CBHW022055020426
42335CB00012B/704